WHAT
IF

What if
I did, but I shouldn't have?
What if
I didn't, but I should have?
What If
I wanted to, but I didn't?

A memoir by

WALTER JOE WALL JR.

ISBN 978-1-0980-8138-6 (paperback)
ISBN 978-1-0980-8139-3 (digital)

Christian Faith Publishing, Inc.
832 Park Avenue
Meadville, PA 16335
www.christianfaithpublishing.com

Printed in the United States of America

To Elizabeth Ann Richards. For her memory and the life she lived. She passed away in 2002. Elizabeth taught the second and third grade at the Miller Perry Elementary School for thirty years. Elizabeth also produced many Christmas plays and taught Sunday school at the churches where I pastored. She was a great help to the Gospel ministry.

Joe & Elizabeth
Early in thier marriage

Contents

Preface

Walter Joe Wall Jr. was born to Walter and Bonnie Mae Fox Wall on January 11, 1929, and was married to Elizabeth Ann Richards on May 28, 1952. His wife died on February 28, 2002. They had one daughter, Robin Hope, who married Gary A. Bagnall. They had one daughter, Carter Grace.

Reverend Wall was ordained to the ministry by the Calvary Baptist Church in Erwin, Tennessee, on March 21, 1954. Before going to Carson-Newman University, the Montview Baptist Church in Morristown licensed him to preach. Reverend Wall has served as a pastor at Chestoa, as music director and interim pastor at Calvary in Erwin, a pastor of Bowmantown, Lovelace, and Hickory Tree, and interim pastor of Sunrise Church. Reverend Wall retired from the Sullivan County school system where he served as attendance supervisor, personnel, and public relations director. He was a principal of the Miller Perry extension (later to be called Colonial Heights Middle School) and taught at the Lynn View Middle School.

Reverend Wall attended Rose Elementary, Sherwood Elementary, Morristown Junior High, and Morristown High School where he played on the 1948 football team. After high school, he attended Carson-Newman University and East Tennessee State University on a football scholarship. He also attended Southeastern Baptist Seminary in Wake Forest, North Carolina, from 1958–1960. He has several hours toward a master's degree in education and is the author of the book *Beyond Your Mountain*, which deals with the loss of a loved one.

Reverend Wall has several hobbies that help him to relax. They are bowling, woodworking, fishing, and gardening. He believes that you will have a happy and successful life if you pray that God's will be done in your life and see love and follow the teachings of Jesus Christ by reading the Holy Bible and living the way it teaches us to live. All the things in life will work out for the best for you. Read Romans 8:28, and you will see what can happen.

Lovelace Miss. Bapt Church

Bowmantown Miss. Bapt Church

Hickory Tree Union Church

Chestoa Missionary Baptist Church

Calvary Baptist Church—Erwin Tennessee, where Bro. Will was Music Director and Intern Pastor, and where he was odained into the Gospel Ministry on March 21, 1954

Acknowledgments

There are several people that I would like to thank for helping me write this book.

I would like to thank my granddaughter, Carter Grace Bagnall, who edited, typed, and gave helpful words along the way, my daughter, Robin Hope, and her husband, Gary Bagnall, for proofreading my words.

I thank Dr. Roy Branson for his help and advice regarding the printing and publication of this book. Dr. Branson has written and published about twenty-five books that can be ordered from his internet web page.

I would like to thank my good friend, Dr. Frank C. Roberts, for helping design the front page of this book and for his editorial suggestions. I say a big THANK-YOU to each and every one who has helped me in any way to accomplish this publication.

Robin, Carter Grace and Gray Bagnall

Introduction

In the beginning of your life, you must have guidance. Where does this guidance come from? The guidance for your life comes from many places and many people. The ones that you are closest to, such as your family and friends, guide you and influence your life in living the most. Many factors are involved in the developing of your personality, principles, and character. What you look at and what you think about all the time are what you will become. It is so important to think about where you are headed and the direction you should take to get your desired goal. One of the main reasons for this book, *What If,* is to guide and to show that there are many roads that you can take in life, and each one of us is traveling on at least one of them. The Bible, God's Holy Word, tells us that "as you think in your hearts, so you are." What you watch, read, and spend your time doing will have a strong effect on who you are and how successful and happy you will become.

In order to get started on the right road, each one needs God's help, and the only way to receive God's help is by believing in the Lord Jesus Christ as your personal Savior. God already knows your talents, your abilities, and your thoughts. God does not force anything on you because He has given you the ability to choose. God will show you and direct you if you are His child. We must trust and obey God in all our ways if we want His guidance. There is one factor that plays an important role in our development all through life. That factor is our attitude toward anything and everything that we do. You must have the right kind of attitude toward your work, your goals, your family and friends, and whatever you do with this life that God has given you.

I want to thank several people for their help, advice, instruction, and inspiration for writing this book. When you need help on anything, you should go to someone that has been there and has done that.

Dr. Roy Branson is one of those people that knows how to write and publish books. Dr. Branson has written almost twenty-five books on many different subjects. Dr. Branson asked me a very important question: Joe, why are you writing this book? The main reason for writing this book is to help and advise young people on how and why to choose the right path for their lives. Always remember that God has a will and a plan for your life. However, God does not just hand it out to you. You must do certain things to receive God's help. The very first thing that you must do is to believe that the Lord Jesus Christ is your personal savior, and start living for Jesus each and every day. When you do this, God adopts you into His family, and you are born again. This is a time of spiritual birth, and your name is written on the Lamb's Book of Life, and you are a child of God forever. Study God's Word to find out all the promises that God has promised to His children.

"What If?"

We all have some *what-ifs* in our lives. What if I had done this or that, how different would my life be? You could have, but you didn't. You did, but you wish you hadn't. You would have if you could have, but you just did not take the chance on things working out for your best interest. Sometimes we must take a risk to accomplish our goals in life. Think about the following poem called "To Risk." The author is William Arthur Ward.

> To laugh is to risk appearing a fool.
> To weep is to risk appearing sentimental.
> To reach out to another is to risk exposing your true self.
> To expose feelings is to risk exploring your true self.
> To place your ideas or dreams before a crowd is to risk their loss.
> To love is to risk not being loved in return.
> To hope is to risk despair.
> To try is to risk failure.
> But risks must be taken because the greatest hazard in life is to risk nothing.
> The person who risks nothing does nothing, has nothing, is nothing.
> He may avoid suffering and sorrow,
> But he cannot learn, feel, change, grow, or live.

Chained by his servitude, he is a slave who
has forfeited all freedom.
Only a person who risks is free.

What If has to do with the living of life and choices we make. What direction you take and the choices you make not only affect you but all people around you. The Bible teaches that what you think about affects who you are and what you will become in life. Choosing the right words to say at the right time to say them is not always easy. I recall, I heard about a minister who was given the opportunity to speak to a prisoner who was about to be electrocuted, and they were walking toward the electric chair. The minister thought about what he could say that would help the prisoner. He wanted to give him words of assurance and comfort. The minister thought maybe he could say, *Peace be with you. God bless you.* But as the prisoner entered the room to be electrocuted, the minister called out, "More power to you."

Sometimes we say the wrong words at the wrong time. Saying yes or no can change a life. The *what-if* thinking doesn't do us any good, unless it helps to change our lives in a more unselfish, effective, and useful way. There is a movie called *It's a Wonderful Life* featuring Jimmy Stewart playing a character named George Bailey. The film is shown around Christmastime. It is hard to resist the humor and optimism found in this film about a family man who is saved by an elderly guardian angel trying to earn his wings. When the world and all our family and friends seem to be against us, we might find ourselves in the same mindset and attitude as George Bailey. When everything is going bad and all of life seems lost, you might feel like saying as George Bailey says, "I wish I had never been born." What if you had never been born? There would be nothing in this life that you had caused to take place and had shared in. They would not be because you have not caused them to be. There would not be that wife or husband to share your life's dreams with. There would not be your children to love and support. There would not be that grand-child to love and support. You have caused so many wonderful things to happen. These things would not be if you were never born.

The twenty-sixth chapter of Matthew tells us of Judas Iscariot betraying Jesus before the chief priest, and in one verse the scripture says that "it had been good for that man if had he not been born." Judas sold Jesus (his love, friendship, and trust) for thirty pieces of silver. There are those today who would sell their friends and family for anything that would help them get what they want. *What if* causes us to ask some questions about life, about living, and the decisions we make. In my life, as in yours, I can think about and reflect upon what if I had accepted some job offers, and I had some that were really good. After I finished high school, I was offered a training and preparation program for the position of manager of the A&P grocery chain, and a beginning salary of $125.00 per week. In 1949, that was a great salary for anyone. When thinking about going to college, I had the choice of going to Furman University and Clemson University and even to a junior college in Arizona. What if I had gone to one of them instead of going to Carson-Newman College and ETSU? What if I had attended Southern Baptist Seminary in Louisville, Kentucky, instead of Southeastern Baptist Seminary in Wake Forest, North Carolina? My ministry might have been different. What if I had accepted the position to be the assistant public relations director with the Tennessee Education Association? What if I had accepted the offer by Reverend Warren Johnson, pastor of Bethel View Baptist Church, to serve as the youth director? What if I had accepted the offer by the principal Lawrence Garland of the Blountville Middle School to become a shop teacher? What if I had accepted the offer by Al Gregory, manager of channel 11 news station, to become their anchor newsman? What if when the Lord called me to the gospel ministry to preach and teach His word, I said no and refused His call?

The Lord had work for me to do, and when He called I said, "Here I am. Send me. Use me." And He has over the years. When you come to the point or crossroads in life to make a choice, what will you do? I believe that God gives a call to each one according to one's God-given abilities and talents. You must answer God's call to you with a yes or no. The Bible says, "Many are called but few are chosen." What does that mean? It means that when you say "Here I am, Lord. Use me in your service and in your kingdom's work," you are chosen by God to serve Him and receive His blessing throughout your life. I believe that God has a purpose, a will, and a plan for each one if we are willing to fit into His will and plan. Always remember that you are making a difference in someone's life for good or for evil. I believe that we need to search and study God's Holy Word, the Bible, and listen for the direction that the Lord would have us take before we act on anything. Proverbs 27:1 says, "Boast not thy self of tomorrow, for thou knowest not what a day may bring forth."

If you want to make God laugh, tell Him what you are going to do tomorrow. We must always remember that God is in charge of everything, and He is in control. Ecclesiastes 3:1 tells us that "To everything, there is a season and a time for every purpose under heaven." You can only have true happiness, joy, and peace of mind when you fit into God's plan and will for your life. God lets you and me make the decision to follow the way He would call us to go. God does not force Himself on anyone, God will call you. He will encourage you in some way and will let you know the way He wants you to go, but you must say "yes, I will" or "no, I will not" follow him. Always live life one moment at a time. The moments go by so fast. The older you get, the faster time goes. When you get past seventy, everyone expects you to say very little and not get in the way of people who are moving faster and faster. Just remember that older people move things along really well. I read somewhere that old folks are worth a fortune with the silver in their hair, the gold in their teeth, the stones in their kidneys, the lead in their feet, and the gas in their stomach. The lady said, "I have become a lot more social with the passing of the years. Some might even call me a frivolous old gal. I'm seeing five gentlemen every day. As soon as I wake up, willpower helps me get out of bed. Then I go see John. Then Charlie Horse comes along. And when he's in the house, he takes a lot of my time and attention. When he leaves, Arthur Ritis shows up and stays the rest of the day. He doesn't like to stay in one place very long, so he takes me from joint to joint. After such a busy day, I'm really tired and glad to go to bed with Ben Gay. What a life I'm living!"

This is really how many older people live. I believe that older people can have a useful and purposeful life if they will trust the Lord and keep serving him and keep their minds and bodies doing something. Whatever our age might be, we need to ask the question *what if?* when we make a decision regarding the living of life because the wrong move or act can cause a lot of heartaches or trouble.

God's Plan

I believe that God has a plan and a will for each person He brings into the world. It makes no difference who your parents are or how you arrived in the world, God loves you and wants you to be a part of His family.

You may ask, how do you know what God's will is for your life? Like the Bible teaches, you must seek His will. Pray for God's will to be done, and He will reveal His will to you. Nothing is going to take place unless you really want it. I do not believe that God forces His will on anyone. God will call you to His service, and you must answer with a yes or no.

I ask myself over and over, "Am I where God wants me, doing what he wants me to do?" If you are living a life that is pleasing to God, you will be happy, and peace will flood your soul. I always knew when I said no to God's calling that I would fall flat on my face in failure, and I would not have peace and contentment in my life. Jesus said, "My peace I give unto you." You cannot have the Jesus Christ kind of peace without Him living in your soul.

When I was about twelve years old, my uncle John preached a message at the Liberty Methodist Church in Morristown. And God called me into His family. And I was born again. My name was written in the Lamb's Book of Life. And I have been trying to live for Jesus ever since. Jesus told Nicodemus, "Ye must be born again" to belong to God's family and live forever.

Hello Brother Joe,

These are the names of the men in this picture:
- Pastor John Kune
- Pastor Mike Womack
- You, Pastor Wall
- Pastor David Crutchfield
- Gray Amos, Music leader

If there was anything else you need please let me know. Praying the Lord bless you will a wonderful Christmas and a Happy, Healthy New Year!

David

School Days

The custom of the first year of school was to attend school in your bare feet. I attended the Rosemont Elementary School in Morristown for the first six years. The school only had five grades. I failed the fifth grade. When I failed, I asked the teacher to change my name from W. J. to Joe, which is my middle name. The teacher honored my request, and I thanked her for it. While in the fifth grade, I was appointed a position of helping students cross from one corner of the street to the other corner as they traveled home from school. I don't remember who it was, but one boy took my position, and I knocked him down because he did. The principal, Miss Katie, called me to her office, and what she told me was life-changing. She said that she could send me to the reforming school for acting like that, and I promised her that I would be a good boy the rest of my life. And I've tried to be just that kind of person.

I attended the Sherwood Elementary School for the sixth grade, which was across town. And after that, I went to the junior high school where Charles Strange was the principal and also the B team football coach. Mr. Strange had a great influence on my life. I went out for football one time, and I didn't like it all that much. I dropped out, and the next day, Mr. Strange saw me at the bowling alley and gave me a swift kick in the rear to get my attention. Mr. Strange told me that he wanted me back out on the football field. I went back and stayed with it through a scholarship in playing football at Carson-Newman College and East Tennessee State University. Charles Strange was highly thought of in Morristown, and the East High School addition was named in his honor. Several of Mr. Strange's students were invited to speak. I considered it an honor to speak on his behalf at the dedication program.

Coach Petie Siler had a great influence on my life. I played on the 1948 football team. Coach Siler invited Coach Howard from Clemson College in South Carolina to speak to our football banquet in 1949, and as a result, Coach Howard invited Tom Pugh and me to try out for a football scholarship. Tom and I started out toward Clemson with the only transportation we had—our thumbs. We spent one night at a friend's house, who were friends with Tom's mom and dad. The next day, we continued on our trip using our thumbs by way of traveling. We were about halfway between Greenville, South Carolina, and Clemson when a big Buick Roadmaster slowed down and picked us up.

As we rode along, the man asked us where we were going. We told him that we were going to Clemson. He slowed his car down and told us to get out and that he could not be taking us to Clemson. We did not know what to say or think. He told us that he was the football coach at Furman. He told us to come by Furman and try out there also.

Tom and I ended up playing for Carson-Newman and later played for East Tennessee State in Johnson City. As we go through life, we have many roads that we can travel on. However, we need to ask God to help us travel on the road that will lead us in the direction that He has planned out for us. I believe what Romans 8:28 teaches which says, "And we know that all things work together for good to them that love God, to them who are called according to his purpose."

The many experiences that we have in life prepare us for the next step and the road that we travel. When I was very young, my dad took me to the Centenary Methodist Church in Morristown, and I was sprinkled to confirm me. And then later, dad took me across town to the Montview Missionary Baptist Church where I was baptized into the fellowship of that church. A Methodist friend, Kenny Ellis, told me in a joking way that I had it covered because I had been baptized both ways. My membership stayed at the Montview Baptist Church for many years. God called me into the ministry at the Montview Church where I served as youth director and music director for several years. After attending Carson-Newman and ETSU, I attended Southeastern Seminary in North Carolina to continue studying for the gospel ministry. God has really blessed me as I have tried to serve him at Chestoa and Calvary in Erwin, Calvary in Bristol, Bowmantown in Jonesboro, Lovelace in Fall Branch, and Sunrise and Hickory Tree in Sullivan County. Today I am only able to do supply and interim work. Growing up in Morristown, I worked at Gluck Brothers Furniture Company factory and Morristown Turning. I worked also for the A&P grocery store and sold insurance for the Life of Georgia Insurance Co.

Ken Pack and Tom Pugh
MHS "Petie" Siler Reunion—July 2008

Love, Courtship, and Marriage

While I was working at the A&P grocery store, I met and fell deeply in love with Elizabeth Ann Richards, later to become my wife. I was also trying my best to serve the Lord at Montview Baptist Church as music director and youth director. I believe that God sent Elizabeth to be my wife because everything worked out so well. God is always looking out for His children who follow His will and teachings. I have always prayed that God's will be done in my life.

I remember sitting in my car at the A&P store when Elizabeth and I were discussing our future. She said that I could get a job like her brother, Delany, had with the telephone company, and we could get married. I told her how much I loved her, but God had called me into the ministry, and I needed to prepare for that. We chose to continue seeing each other. Elizabeth grew up in Bristol, Tennessee, and her father was a builder. He was sent to Morristown to build some houses.

God is always moving and doing things in our lives when we do not even know it.

Elizabeth's family lived close to the A&P store where I worked. Each day Mrs. Richards would send Elizabeth to the store for her daily vegetables. I would see Elizabeth enter the store, and I would make sure that no one waited on her except me. My heart would start beating a little faster when I saw Elizabeth coming my way, and I wanted to marry her. It was love at first sight in the summer of 1948.

When school started that fall, I wanted to ask Elizabeth for a date to a football game, but I did not even know her name. Elizabeth had a friend who was also a friend of mine. I asked that friend, Margaret Riggs, to ask Elizabeth if she would go with me to the football game. Elizabeth said yes, and we had our first date. It was a B team football game, which was played on a Thursday night. I played on the first team, which was played on Friday night, and I asked her for a date on Friday and Saturday. From that time forth, we dated on a steady basis. Elizabeth's father was sent to work on another project in Knoxville, Tennessee. The family moved to Fountain City, which is just outside of Knoxville. I visited them many times when I was courting Elizabeth.

About 1950, Mr. Richards moved his family back to Bristol where he built his house at 101 Dairy Circle Drive where Elizabeth and I were to live with them until Elizabeth died in 2002. Our courtship continued from 1948 until 1950 when we got engaged to be married.

God always knows what is best for us if we will just put our faith and trust in Him. Jesus will guide you through any problem that you might have.

In those early days when Elizabeth and I were going to college, I had no way to travel except by thumb. On one occasion, I used my thumb to come to Bristol for a visit with Elizabeth. On this visit, I became very sick in my stomach. Elizabeth's dad took us to the Greyhound bus station, and I got on the bus to return to Morristown. I was so tired and sick that I fell asleep and never knew when the bus left Bristol. When I woke up, the bus was in Knoxville. I missed the bus stop in Morristown.

During our courtship of about five years, we had very few problems. It was a great and wonderful time. Elizabeth was in school at Virginia Intermont College while I was in and out of Carson-Newman College in Jefferson City, Tennessee, on a football scholarship during the 1950–51 season.

When you are in love with a person, you want the very best life has to offer for that person, and you love that person with all your heart, soul, and body. I can say that Elizabeth and I had that kind of love for each other. I always tell couples I marry that it is not how you start out but how you end up. And that has proven to be so true with the living of life.

On May 28,1952, Elizabeth and I got married at Calvary Baptist Church in Bristol, Tennessee. Reverend Ben Holdman performed the ceremony. He was a good friend and pastor of my home church in Morristown, Tennessee. We did not have a big formal wedding; however, we did have a great wedding. We stood in front of the church altar and made our commitment to each other. Only the minister and Elizabeth's family attended. After our wedding, Mrs. Richards had a reception at their house, which lasted about three hours. Elizabeth and I left for our honeymoon trip shortly after the reception. We headed to the Smokey Mountains and took the route through Kingsport, Fall Branch, Greeneville, and Newport. In Kingsport, we had a flat. And in Newport, we stayed to eat, and I thought I locked my keys up in the car. I broke a vent window to get my keys only to find that the car door was unlocked all the time. We had a great honeymoon in the Smoky Mountains.

Our love continued to grow all through the years. I tell the ones I marry that your love never stands still. You are growing in your love, and it takes an effort to grow. You must work at loving each other. I've found that love grows stronger and more precious with the little things that we do for one another, like being considerate of one another's feelings, helping each other solve a problem, sharing your interests, not letting your differences of opinion spoil your relationship, and showing respect for one another.

After we got married, we continued our education at ETSU. We had a small apartment with Mr. and Mrs. Rogers, which was almost on the campus of ETSU. Elizabeth finished college before I did and got a teaching job with the Sullivan County school system. She taught the second and third grade at Miller Perry Elementary School for the next thirty-four years.

While I was finishing ETSU and playing football, I was called to be music director and assistant minister for the Calgary Baptist Church in Erwin, Tennessee. My responsibly would be to direct the music program at Calgary and be the pastor of their mission in the Chestoa community. Elizabeth just fell in love with the people of Calvary and Chestoa. God really blessed our efforts at both places. We helped the Chestoa mission become a church and worked with the Calvary Church. One weekend, Elizabeth and I went to Louisville, Kentucky, to check on attending the Southern Missionary Baptist Seminary. And while I was in Louisville, the pastor resigned, and his duties became my responsibility for the next year, in addition to directing the music program of the church.

Elizabeth really helped me in many ways. She was the adult ladies' Sunday school teacher. I believe God has a way of turning something bad into something good, which will be according to His will and purpose. As a result of all that took place, I became the interim pastor of Calvary and continued to carry out my many duties as music director. I was also pastor of Chestoa Baptist Church at the same time. We helped organize Chestoa mission into a church, and I became their first pastor. God really blessed our efforts. I believe that God will bless our efforts when we try to serve Him and do His will.

While serving the Calvary and Chestoa churches, I was also employed by the Sullivan County education system. I have worked in several different positions, including attendance supervisor, principal of Miller Perry annex (later to be called Colonial Heights Middle School), personal and public director, and industrial arts teacher of Lynn View Middle School. After retirement, I have filled in at the Colonial Heights Middle School and East High School. I have faith to believe that God takes care of His children. If you have been born again of the spiritual birth, you belong to God's family. And He will take care of you. And He will never leave you.

After serving at Calvary and Chestoa churches, we felt it was time to continue my preparation for the ministry. I attended Southeastern Seminary in Wake Forest, North Carolina, and classes were held on Tuesday through Friday. This was scheduled that way to give students the opportunity to minister to churches over the weekend. I came home on Friday and went back on Monday. Because of the long weekend, I served the Calvary Baptist Church in Bristol as their music director while I attended school in Wake Forest. After two and one-half years of attending seminary at Wake Forest, I was called as a pastor of the Philadelphia Baptist Church near Jonesboro, which was later changed to Bowmantown Baptist Church.

God really blessed our work in Bowmantown. We were blessed with a little baby girl named Robin Hope while at Bowmantown, and we had the wonderful privilege of leading the church into full-time ministry. Elizabeth and I severed Bowmantown church until a vote was taken to show the keeping or rejecting of having me as their pastor. I had told the church many times that if there was any outward objection for us being there that we would be gone. I won the election, but I lost some of the members that voted against me, and we left.

Shortly after we left, the Lovelace Baptist Church of Fall Branch called us to serve them as their pastor. I accepted their invitation and stayed for almost thirty years. When God closes one door, He always opens another one where we can serve Him. I always ask myself the question, "Am I where God wants me to be, doing what God wants me to do?" If I am, I know that I am going to be happy and have joy in my heart and soul.

There was so much work to be accomplished at both churches. The Bowmantown church had no water, no baptistery, and no Sunday school departments. The church only met two times a month. I told the deacons that I would be there every Sunday. Bill Bowman and Bengi, his son, drove me around the community and showed me the possibility for growing the church. Bill said that I could get another church, but I said that I would come every Sunday, and that's the way it worked out.

I believe that God has a place and a time for each of us to accomplish His work, and we need to find our place. I believe that it is very important to know why you are doing what you are doing. Is it for your benefit? Or is it to serve or help someone else? God has a way of moving us along in His work if we are willing to seek His will for our lives.

I feel like many things that happened at the Bowmantown church helped to move the church forward. The church moved from being a part-time church to a full-time church and provided a pastor's home. We have many happy memories of the Bowmantown church family. One of the happiest memories happened in 1962 when out daughter, Robin Hope, was born. Many other wonderful events occurred, and we have many dear friends at the Bowmantown church and community.

When I resigned at Bowmantown, the Holston Baptist Associate Missionary, Reverend Paul Hall, called me and asked me if I might be interested in pastoring Lovelace Baptist Church in Fall Branch, Tennessee. I accepted the call to the Lovelace Church in 1966 and served them for almost thirty years. I believe that God has a place for each one to serve Him if you are willing to seek His will and purpose for your life.

There was much more to accomplish at the Lovelace Church. After about ten years serving the Lovelace Church, helping put water in the church, and a new addition added, I felt that my work was finished, and I resigned. Little did I know that the church would burn to the ground within the next three months, and we all would be standing there watching it burn with tears in our eyes. The chairman of the deacons, Foster Taylor, came to me, put his arms around me, and asked, "Preacher, would you come back and help us build the church back?"

"You know," I said, "I would be happy to do all that the Lord will lead me to do. God really blessed our efforts in building and working together for a new church."

With the help and efforts of the Baptist association, many churches, many individuals, and the church membership, the church was built back and fully paid for, and a dedication of the church to God was conducted in less than one year. It takes each person doing what their talents will let them do to carry a church along the way. Each person, making an effort, will help the church move forward. The Lovelace Church had the 125th homecoming celebration on June 27, 2004. Reverend Joe Hensley became the pastor, and I stayed on to chair the homecoming and History committees. We had thirteen members of the History committee, and each had an assignment to accomplish. Each person made a great effort, and LaWanda Baskett was a leading member and was responsible for the publication of the history book. God really blessed our efforts at Lovelace, and we give Him all the praise and Glory.

When I finished the seminary in Wake Forest, I got my job back as the attendance supervisor for the Sullivan County school system, which lasted for nineteen years. In 1977, the superintendent of schools, Paul Nelson, and the school board promoted me to the new position of personal and public relations director for the Sullivan County school system. In this position, I interviewed 1,800 people for possible employment in the school system. This position lasted about five years until a new superintendent of schools was elected. Many changes were made concerning the positions and the courses that were taught, which a lot of staff and teachers thought was not needed and was unnecessary. I was moved to teaching shop at the Lynn View Middle School, which included the sixth, seventh, and eighth grades.

One day I got a call from the new superintendent who wanted to move me again. This time, I was to be teaching math to the sixth graders. I called him with the determination that I was not going to move again, and I would see him in court. That was the last I heard about any more changes that I would have to make. I believe the Bible when it teaches that God will take care of His children and will be with them throughout life. I can truly say that God has taken care of me all through my life.

I retired from the school system in 1987, and shortly after that, the Lynn View School closed. It would be a great thing if we only knew what to say and do to make the future turn out like we wanted. The best thing that you can do is to put your faith and trust in the Lord Jesus Christ and let Him guide you in the path and direction that is best for you. We need to pray that God's will be done in our life. On many occasions, I wish that I had prayed more instead of acting on my own. I look back on my life and wonder why God let certain things happen to me and why I made certain decisions. I can also look back and see where God has carried me through many difficult situations. We must always remember that God has a reason and a purpose for anything and everything that happens to His children.

As I look back on my life, I can truly say that God has guided me every step of the way.

I grew up in a very poor neighborhood where the whites and blacks lived very close to each together. We lived together with respect for one another and lived with peace in our hearts. This was before the desegregation movement by Martin Luther King Jr. I was the oldest of five children. One little brother, Johnathan, died when he was about three months old. I will never forget Momma screaming early one morning saying that he was dead. I was only about eleven years old, but I can hear that scream.

As parents, we need to teach our children to live by the principles of the Bible, and we need to live before them the way we would like for them to grow up and become. About ninety percent of the children grow up to be just like their parents. We know nothing when we are born. It is very important that we have good training, good instruction, and a good education if we are to become productive citizens and have a happy and successful life. What children hear, read, and look at, and who they associate with make a great impact on who they become and who they really are. I read somewhere that if you want to fly like an eagle, don't fly with the buzzards. That is so true because people put you in the same class as the ones that you fly with.

The Call to Service

I believe that regardless of what a person chooses to do in life that there must be a motivating force that pulls you in that direction. That motivating force is lacking in many homes today.

As parents, we must teach and motivate our children. If a mother or father lies, cheats, steals, curses, has no regard or respect for those in authority, is selfish, will not work, is always taking and never giving, does not ever attend church, is always critical of anything and everything, has no ambition at all, and has a bad attitude, you—as a parent—can expect your children to turn out just like you. Everyone has some kind of attitude. It is up to you to develop the right kind of attitude. You can have a good or bad attitude, you can have a "don't care" attitude, sad or happy attitude that starts your day. The one thing that you should know is that you are in charge of the kind of attitude that you have. Many times, it is my reaction to something that causes my attitude to change. I believe that two of the most important factors for the development of a good and happy life are motivation and attitude. These two factors help us to decide and determine what path in life we want to take. Many people motivate us along life's highway, so one thing I believe is lacking in the development and growing up of our children of the twenty-first century is giving a child some type of responsibility. We should teach them to love and respect one another. The Bible teaches us to even love our enemies and those who disrespectfully use us. Trying to live according to the teaching of God's Holy Word is not always easy. When I accepted God's call into the gospel ministry, He led me to serve Him at the Calvary Baptist Missionary Church and their mission in Erwin, Tennessee, where I was ordained in 1954. After seminary training, God called me to serve at several churches. Among the churches where I have served are Calvary Baptist Church in Bristol, Bowmantown Church near Jonesboro, Lovelace Church in Fall Branch, Sunrise Baptist Church, and Hickory Tree Church in Sullivan County.

I feel that God has guided me and led me all the way in the work that He has called me to accomplish. If you seek, you will find. If you knock, it will be opened to you what God's will and plan for your life should be. I still try to serve the Lord by filling in at churches that need a pastor, or the pastor is on vacation or is sick. God has truly blessed this type of ministry. We must always keep learning and serving and never give up on the living of the kind of life God has called us to live.

What Time Is It?

God's Holy Word teaches that there is a time for all things. What time do you have to accomplish the plans you have for living the life that God has given us? We only have so much time appointed to each of us. The scientists are really funny about the keeping of time. At the end of 2016, the space flight center in Maryland added an extra second to the end of the year. They did that because the rotation of earth slows down over time. The year just got a little bit longer.

You might ask, "Well, what difference does it make anyways?" It might not make much difference to you or me, however, to the person launching a spaceship into orbit around the world, every second counts. What are you doing with your time? We must spend our time wisely. Several things help us to spend our time wisely or unwisely. Our attitude has much to do with how and why we spend our time in certain way. Always remember, you set the tone of your day by the attitude you have when you get up in the morning. You are in charge of the attitude you have. Don't blame someone else or even the circumstance that you find yourself in. There are some people that blame the past for the problems they have and their attitude of self-pity. We must remember that the past is forever gone, and we must live in the present and plan for the future. Time passes so fast that whatever we are going to do, we must not put it off, but do it now. I read the following, and I think it is so true: I shall pass this way but once. Any good thing, therefore, that I can do, or any kindness that I can show, let me do it now. Let me not defer nor neglect it for I will not pass this way again.

I believe that it is so important as to what a person reads, hears, or looks at, or thinks about. What you think about all the time is what you become. There are three kinds of people in the world: those who watch things happen, those who make things happen, and those who have no idea what happens. There are all kinds of communications in the world today, and it is so important how we let them influence our thinking. The Bible teaches us that what a person thinks in their heart is what kind of person they are going to be. Time is so important because it goes by so fast, and we must make the best use of our time. There is a time of learning and a time for putting to good use what we have learned. I believe that there is a time and place for all things to take place. I pray that each person may use their time wisely.

Joe & Elizabeth Wall
Eva & H.W. Richards

End of Life's Journey

Ecclesiastes, the third chapter, teaches us that "to everything, there is a season, and a time to every purpose under the heaven." I believe that everything and every action in the living of life has a time and place to occur. I believe that when you are born, God is looking after you with His tender, loving care until you come to the age of accountability. When you come to the age of accountability, you will know right from wrong, and at that age, you become a sinner and will be responsible for your sins and will have to answer for all of your actions before Almighty God. The Bible teaches us that there is a time to be born and a time to die. The time you live from birth to death will be wonderful if you have Jesus as your Lord and Savior, and He is guiding your living of the life that He has given you.

I was born on January 11, 1929 and accepted Jesus as my Savior at about the age of twelve. Jesus has guided my life ever since that time. Now I am getting very close to the end of life's journey, and I praise God and thank Him every day for all His blessings, His guidance, and His love that He has shown toward me. We should think of each day as an adventure to serve the Lord Jesus Christ and others that are in need. If we think only of ourselves and of no one else, we will live a life that is very selfish, unfulfilling, and unrewarding. God's Holy Word encourages us to be a caring, loving, and useful individuals. And if you are that kind of person, God will greatly bless you all the days of your life. There is a poem written by Linda Ellis that I have used many times when I was called on to conduct a funeral, and it's called "How Do You Live Your Dash."

I read of a man who stood to speak at a funeral of a friend.

He told of the dates on her tombstone from the beginning to the end.

He noted that first came her date of birth and spoke of the following date with tears. But he said what mattered most of all was the dash between those years.

For that dash represents all the time that she spent alive on earth, and now only those who loved her know what that small line is worth.

It matters not how much we own, the cars, the house, the cash. What matters is how we live and love and how we spend our dash.

So think about this long and hard, are there things you'd like to change? For you never know what time is left that still can be rearranged.

If we could just slow down enough to consider what's true and real and always try to understand the way people feel.

And be less quick to anger and show appreciation more, and love the people in our lives like we've never loved before.

We could treat each other with respect and more often wear a smile. Remembering that this special dash might only last a little while.

So when your eulogy's being read with your life's actions to rehash, would you be proud of the things they say about how you lived your dash?

Alone, Grieving, and Moving On

When you lose someone that you have loved and lived with most of your life, it is not very easy to move on with your life. The living of life changes with every passing day. Many people give you advice as to what you should do, however, only you can make that choice. The Bible, God's Holy Word, is a great source of comfort and instruction during this period of time in your life. The third chapter of Ecclesiastes is a good place to start reading in the Bible. Ecclesiastes 3:1–4 says, 'To everything, there is a season and a time to every purpose under the heaven—a time to be born, and a time to die; a time to plant, and a time to pluck up that which is planted; a time to kill, and a time to heal; a time to break down, and a time to build up; a time to weep, and a time to laugh; a time to mourn, and a time to dance."

You must remember that you, and only you, are in charge of your life and how you go through your grief. You must give yourself time to heal. You must deal with your feelings and emotions. Your feelings may take the form of crying, of being sad, of being depressed, of being angry, or of feeling that you are alone. No one can understand how you feel except someone that has gone through what you are experiencing. It always helps to keep your mind and body active. The expression "if you don't use it you will lose it" is so very true. It is always good to plan for the future.

One widow wrote me and said, 'There is a time for mourning, but there is also a time to pull yourself together and go on with life. Stay busy, there is so much to do if you have the heart and will."

I don't believe God wants us to feel sorry for ourselves and to wallow in self-pity. Although I have my memories, I just don't let myself dwell on them. You must do all you can to move on with your life. The following principle of life has helped me so very much:

I shall pass this way but once. Any good thing that I can do, or any kindness that I can show, let me do it now.

Let me not defer it or neglect it, for I shall not pass this way again.

Oct. 1982
L to R
Joe Wall, Vaughm Brewer
Roy Moore, Paul Nelson

State Bowling
Bowling
L to R
Wall, Jones and Hyatt

State Tenn.
Bowling medals Mr. Wall has won

About the Author

The Reverend Walter Joe Wall, Jr. was born in Morristown, Tennessee, and attended Morristown High School, Carson-Newman College, and graduated from East Tennessee State University. After graduation, Reverend Wall attended Southeastern Seminary and was ordained in 1954. Over the next sixty-five years, he served as the pastor of numerous churches, including Chestoa Baptist Church (Unicoi County, Tennessee), Bowmantown Baptist Church (Bowmantown, Tennessee), Lovelace Baptist Church (Fall Branch, Tennessee), and Hickory Tree Union Church (Sullivan County, Tennessee).

CPSIA information can be obtained
at www.ICGtesting.com
Printed in the USA
LVHW070439270721
693794LV00008B/135

9 781098 081386